Just a Boy Blaming Himself

Daniel Hess

© 2021 Daniel Hess

Book cover designed by Alejandro Estrada

All rights reserved. This book or any portion thereof may not be reproduced or used in any manner whatsoever without the express written permission of the publisher except for the use of brief quotations in a book review.

Table of Contents

Part 1: Home or a close approximation therein 1

Trim 3
Sitting Down 4
Dream 5
Open Walls 6
Music 7
Night Stares 8
Sleep 9
Call Me 10
Hot Room 11
I Like Me Like This 12
TV 13
Grandma 14
Not Sure 15
Scare Me 16
Accident 17
Centimeter 19
Stale Cigarettes 20
It Feels Like Heaven 21
Timeless Summer 22
Summer Sun 23
Home 24
Smell 25
Positivity 26
Cocoon 27
Empty 28
Silence 29
Beast 30
Time Capsule 31
Regression 32
TV Screen 33
Icebox 34
Purple Haze 35
Bridge 36
Avalanche 37
Mundane Motions 38
Reflections 39
Red Husk 40
Cacophony 41

Not Myself	42
Home	43
Technologically Shamed	44
Trash Day	46
Sleep Well	47

Part 2: Work or an incompletion of progress 49

Weddings	51
This Week	52
At A Wedding	54
Vacation	56
Crying Outside of a Taco Bell	58
Lines	59
Young Artists	60
Cycles	61
Art	62

Part 3: Sex or some kind of release 63

Girls	65
Bliss	66
Late Night Caller	67
Sheets	68
How Many Times	69
Dance with Me	70
Middle-Aged Woman	72
Naked on the Beach	73
IDK	74
Ghost Ship	75
Seek Me Out	76
Horror	78
Sugar Rush	79
Avert	81
Frustration	83
Touching Needs	85
Sex and Love	86

Part 4: Death and all the consequences as a result 87

Heroes	89
Toenail	90
Consume	91
Why	92
Anxiety	93
Grow	94
Float On	95

Sparrow	96
Stray Bullet	98
Little Worm	100
Emotional Misunderstanding	101
Festival Vibes	102
I Miss	103
Lexi	105
Dance Around Little Girl	107
Demographics	108
Dreams	110
Steal Me Away	111
Judgement Days	113
Circle	114
Moon Sky	116
Toy	117
See You	118
Die	119
Repeat	120
Time Stamps	121
Self Death	122
God	123
250 Dollars	124
Iron	125
Days with Lauren	126
Change (Or Lack Thereof)	127
Thinking Back	128
Acid Stain	129
Growth	130

Part 5: Love and the complicated balance of life 131

Facial Structure	133
Candle	134
True Love	135
Tired	136
So Close	137
Hypnotic Call	138
Responsibility	140
Take	141
Text Me	142
True Dreams	143
Party Girl	144
Last Night	146
Woman with a Ring	147

Pink Haired Girl in Walmart	148
Fingertips	149
Letters You Wrote	150
Hello Dolly	151
In A Target	152
Years Ago	154
Predictions	155
The Movies	156
Dream State	157
Inspire	159
Generations	160
Leech	162
Mountain of Doubt	163
Text Poetry	164
Companionship	165
Go Away	166
My Time	167
At the Movies	168
You, her, she, it, me, my, love	169
Blood Rush	170
You Were A Doll	171
Ruse	172
Swear	173
Family	174
Let it be known	175
Skateboard Girl	176
30 Years	177
Bittersweet Berries	178
Repeated Listening	179
Pain Love Pain	180
Crash Lips	181
Go get fucked up	182
Waves	183
Longing for Motion	184
Yellow Dye	185
Part 6: This is it, the closing part	**187**
An Ending	189

Foreword

I've known Daniel since he was six. We have been kayaking and going to the movies often, since that time. What I am trying to say is, I've known him for a long time. Daniel speaks from his heart, almost to a fault. His book of poems speaks mostly from the sad places in his heart. Some of these poems are raw, a bit edgy and may seem harsh at times. This acknowledges his vulnerability.

Being a psychotherapist, I often want my patients to journal; to write down how they feel. I use this to help them with self-awareness. Daniel has much self-awareness and as Dorothy Parker stated, "Art is a form of catharsis." I feel that Daniel, through his poetry, has been able to bring across what a lot of us actually feel. When reading this book of poems, one gets to see a part of Daniel not many are allowed to see.

--David Quade LCSW-C

Thank you to all of those who listened to my musings on late night texts. Thank you to everyone who ever said that I had any semblance for writing. Thank you to anyone who inspired me good or bad to put these feelings down on paper.

Most of all thank you for picking this book up today and taking even a slight moment to read my silly poems.

-Daniel Hess 1/30/2021

Part 1:

Home
or a close approximation
therein

Trim

Tonight, I saw these pieces of trim on the wall
And I had to tear them down
I saw the kindness you had put into them
Fixing them up
Painting them pretty
But I knew it was all a lie
Convenient love that you felt
Turned to hatred after we parted

They were laughing at me nailed to the wall
Feeling permanent in their placement
So, I tore them off to scream shut up

They are quiet now
Laying in a pile in the backyard

Sitting Down

She sat down and felt the weight of the world
Bringing her down every night
She couldn't keep from crying

She wanted to hear the phone ring
But the call never came
Maybe tomorrow

Or it won't be the same

Dream

I had this dream we were living together
There was a woman watching you though
You hated her
Dug up dirt

She slowly mixed pills into your drink
Every day
Just in case

One day you confronted her
Had all the facts laid out
I watched it unfold from the kitchen

She stuck you in the neck and in the spine
You shut down
Were mindless

I wanted to do something I screamed your name
Then I woke up
Birds chirping

You haven't been in this house for years
Why do I care?
Why are you still here?

Open Walls

Some walls open
Some walls closed

I like the space
But crave the structure

Half undone
Yet half complete

Do I ever want this project to finish?

Do I want to feel a gentle breeze?

Music

Loud sounds hit my ears

Make me forget all the problems

Louder please

High energy beeps
Boops

Stop and dance
Step in unison

Scream at the top of my lungs

Serotonin spilling all over

Song's over
Play another quick

I can hear things coming back to focus

Night Stares

I like to keep the lights off

So, I can look at the world knowing it can't see me

It feels so much more natural

Watching those who cannot see me

Sleep

No sleep
No rest

In bed
Now rest

Now sleep
Now bed

Manic mind
Lost thoughts

Transform a time
Lost thoughts

No to hold
No to have

Broken fragments
Bewildered sheets

Broken dreams
Tiny pieces

Where are the dead
When do they rise?
Another nightmare
Another surprise

How do I end you?
Maybe just here

Call Me

I want my ex-girlfriend to call me
So she can say sorry and I can too

I wish I could get a true resolution
To all the issues we had

Maybe you could tell me where I went wrong
And I could shed some tears

That would be nice
But I had a thousand chances to get that closure

Instead I spent it pretending
That we were going to get back together

And each time it didn't happen
I became a bit more bitter

Then all was lost
But time has passed

Can we just be adults now?
Talk it out for a little while?
Maybe?

Hot Room

In a hot room
Shadows on the wall

Thinking of the times we had
Are you doing the same?

Down in Peachtree City
In your parent's basement

Probably not
But in your mind, I am dwelling

When really, I am just remembering
All the good you brought me

I don't want you back
I mean I did a little bit

But you made it obvious you were done
And I respect that

I just want you to be doing ok
I hate how I hurt you

I was a child
Staring at dark walls
In a hot room

I Like Me Like This

This is the me I like
The one so high he can't stress about life

This is the me I like
Floating above anything without a care

I want to be high forever
No like seriously high forever

I want to see everything through broken glasses
None of the pieces making sense

Because it would be easier
It would be better

I really want that
I really want to be high

No more grasping at these straws
No more trying so hard

Just let me free
Let me go

TV

All the lights on in each home
TV shining images into their brains

I wish they could all do more
Achieve higher things

The goals of the world could be bigger
The change could be better

But we distract ourselves
I just want it to be better

Grandma

Grandma are you ok?
Yes, Daniel, are you?

I wish I could say yes but there is something…
What is it?

I just wish you were really here
But I am always there with you, now what's wrong?

I am lost in this world, I'm an outsider from friend groups, I am not seeing anyone, my finances are a mess
But stop for a second

What is it?
I know these are things you don't have but look at all you do have

I know but…
But there is no more to it you will be fine Daniel

Grandma?

Not Sure

I feel like I look good
But no one I think is good likes me

I think I have an ok style
But no one critical really tells me if I do

I think I know my type
But I take what I can get

I am not sure where to go from here
But what I am doing clearly isn't working

Scare Me

I want something to terrify me
A pinch in the night
A whisper in the dark

At least it would be a feeling
And a way to have some emotion

Maybe I would break down
And cry
That would be nice

It would be a release
To take my mind off things
Make me think of you

But no such luck
It's safe here
Until it isn't anymore

Then I will be gone

Accident

I hit a car today

I did all I could to swerve out of the way

The road was too slick

I had nowhere to turn and it happened

I don't remember what I was thinking

In that moment

So many things just flashed around

It was surreal

I wanted to talk to the people

But they immediately wanted to blame me

So, a line was drawn

Why does it have to be that way?

A system in place to make us behave erratically

Like little children

But who knows

Maybe it would be different if I was at fault

But my car is a mess
It will take some time to be fixed

And now I sit and wait
To see what will happen

And go through the trials of insurance
Wish it could be different

But here I am
Outside of Philly

Wishing I was just back home
Back where this didn't happen

Centimeter

Passive pentameter
Passive pentameter

Pass on centimeter
Pass on centimeter

I love the voice
You protect
If only to protect
Your innocent soul

I wanted polly to share his crackers
And crack her shell
Wide open so I could eat again

I'm so hungry
It's been days
Now I'm seeing haze
When I stand too quickly

Prickly leaves scratch my eyes
Until they bleed a crimson tidal force of red
A tidal force of pressure under my ears

Pop pop pop pop
Thanks the pain is gone
Until it starts again
Come here come heal come here come heal

Stale Cigarettes

Stale cigarettes
Stale cigarettes
Stale cigarettes

Get me through the day
Too broke for a pack
Too lazy to scrounge the change
Keep the pace going
Pack up my bags
Going to Seattle
To find your ghost
Tell me what to do

Huffing compressed air
Huffing compressed air
Huffing compressed air

So high so high might see you there
Unless the trigger won't fire
And I'm still here tomorrow

Just one more breath of stale cigarettes
Stale cigarettes
Stale cigarettes

It Feels Like Heaven

Sleeping with no sheets on
The hot air surrounding my skin
It feels like heaven

It's perfectly akin to all the ways
I enjoy this palace of solitude

So glad you are gone
So glad to be alone
It feels like heaven

Sprinkle in some interaction
Makes me feel whole

All I need is music and movies
And a small little house
It's so nice in my head

I wish you could be here
But glad that you aren't

As I lay down, cuddling a pillow
It's the same as a person
It feels like heaven

Timeless Summer

It was a summer of time
Time was endless
We walked around our neighborhoods
Catching all the sun's rays
It was never too hot
We just went
With no destinations in mind
Scraping money together for crap food
Listening to music however we could
I can't remember a single conversation
But it was so wonderful
You were a rock star to me
And a dear friend
The cliché thought is true
That it was truly a simpler time

Summer Sun

I have been dreading this day
All summer long

The cold air passing through my skin
Tearing past my bones

I am never ready
I am never ready

The isolation only made more severe
Since standing outside my door is so unpleasant

I can't just bask in the warm air of summer nights
Sweating on my sheets

I can't just freely ride my bike
Without feeling miserable at every push of my pedal

Winter's chill is a foul beast
I wish I could escape

Summer is the only season I need

Home

Do you know what it is like

To be locked away in a house of memories

Every inch covered in nostalgia

Battling the want to regress

While still moving forward

I could be held

I could be sustained

But would I be alive?

Surrounded by walls of old

I should just tear you down

But it is too late

I have patched you together

Like some kind of monster

Old meets need

New meets old

Hobbled together heaps of plaster over old joints

You want to die

But I am not here to be your savior

Rather, I occupy your fractured core

Staring into nothingness

One more generation of life

Then maybe you can have our sweet release

But not until I die

Smell

I smelled a new section of my sheets tonight

They gave me an intoxication reminiscent of the opposite sex

It was transcendently magical in the way my mind wanted to be choked by it

I could stop breathing air so that my lungs could drown in it

I thought it smelled of a fresh kiss from the lips of someone I hadn't met yet but knew

It was new but not you it was who I wanted to be true

Next time maybe I would be able to let me choke a little more

Positivity

I have so much genuine love for the world
I really love so many people
And I want to always think the best of humanity
You are all capable of so many great things I know it
I know that great things can happen
We are all capable of immense change
And that will happen

Cocoon

I could lay here all day
In this cocoon of warmth
The only light the screen from this phone
It would be easy
Burying myself away from the world
I wonder what it would like if I did
Find me at the start of spring
Like some kind of creature of hibernation
Eyes hollowed out
Skin now mushy
Bones cracking from lack of movement
I would be warm at least
I would be rested
It would be peaceful

Empty

I really shut out the world today
Because everyone shut me out
Every person I opened up to stop talking
They didn't have to say much
Just something besides nothing
So I am trying to sleep the day away
Forget it ever happened
Too bad it did and I am on this couch
What path am I taking?
It all feels pointless
It all feels worthless
I feel like a void
I am empty

Silence

My voice is silent
It makes no sound
I scream aloud
But no one around
You look right at me
But yet past my eyes
I see who you are
But can you see me?
I'm easy to ignore
When no sounds emanate

Beast

There used to be a beast here
A creature inside these walls
Independently dependent
Time has passed
Now a memory
Wish I had the burden
It would be a task
Something to break up the monotony
However, you're gone
It could be a simple replacement
No, that isn't the answer
There just won't be another you

Time Capsule

Looking at things through the lens of a time capsule

Is dangerously innocent

I see a former love

In a snapshot

And feel as though I can reach out to touch that moment of time

But that time has passed

And she has moved far on from that place I see printed on paper

I wish I could stop the need to look back

Nights alone

It's not healthy

Regression

I have regressed

To an infantile state

Sucking the lack of knowledge away from you

Melting the thoughts into mush

So that it can be slurped back

I shouldn't have contacted you

It was so dumb to think anything more of less would come from words on a page

I am just some weak scum

Just some dumb fool weak in my heartache

My self-created loneliness

Which could be cured by simply getting into the car

I can't do it though, I can't go there

They are all just places that remind me of a lifetime spent with someone else

TV Screen

We didn't talk much growing up
Expressing feelings through what we watched
Each show could be a portal to our soul
The language of our hearts on a flickering screen

Instead of a hug I saw it right there
Reaching out to me
I knew my parents cared
But the physical side didn't come

It was a comfort, though
Losing myself in each new story
Making it all seem possible
Making it all seem probable

I miss that warm glow
Soothing me to sleep

Icebox

In my icebox I lament
Thinking backwards, forwards, and in the present
Fields of warm sun lift me up
Dreams of summer night bring me down

I count each passing day to run
Away from these barren walls
Hope to never feel the bitter chill
Beyond that spell of time I'm here

Purple Haze

The world reeks of weed
I can smell it in its unwashed pores
Stumbling into distractions
Witnessing nothing of merit

We hobble into our darkness
Declaring our defeat
At the hands of something within control
But yet we give it all up

To hide from a few scary thoughts
Replaced by pink clouds of comfort
Taking away our wrinkles
Neurons losing connection

Why did we let some haze
Destroy everything so holy?
Why did we let some haze
Take away our true freedom?

Bridge

I heard you couldn't breathe
But that's okay
Me neither
My lungs are full of dust
Most likely from the drywall

It's the home I'm rebuilding
The one without your soul
I wish it wasn't so empty
But all I need is this hole

Hope you are happy
Living across the bridge
It's a safe distance for sure
Far away from these kids

Avalanche

Stepping forwards
While walking backwards
Letting the memories consume me
It's a place I need to go to

My blanket of snow
Avalanche of breath
It doesn't matter where that sensation goes
As long as it gets me high

Mundane Motions

The days are filled with mundane motions
The nights are filled with weeping willows
In between I hold my breath
Hoping to not fill a lung
With the fluid of my suspicion
Deep upon your wicked tongue

I could fill the void with empty baskets
Or treats designed to die and rot
You might not like them for a moment
But it is all for not

May the sun burn bright and fast
Pushing bodies into shadow
If the prophetic notion does not come to pass
Maybe off kilter words will make all the difference

Reflections

I tried looking down the mountainside
And I realized I was blind
I tried staring through the clock on the wall
And I realized it was time

As I overanalyzed, I knew what I would find
Only to end up where it began-deep within my mind

Red Husk

Reflecting back
Is a distorted image
One I wish I could forget
But it begs to be seen

It is the only way to change
Peeling open every scar
It's a red pulsating husk
Where I used to stand

Don't touch it
Might get infected
Or maybe ingested
Long enough to be entranced by its appearance

I never spoke a word
You said it would be ok
Here I am with open arms
A shattered mirror away from redemption

Cacophony

Cacophony save me
Make all other noise obsolete

Only then will my ears bleed so sweetly
Silence begins to swallow them whole

Thank you for this gift
The echoes in my mind

Will reverberate for all time
Heard of Nothing

Today I had no distractions of the mind
No escape from the unexpected
I heard not but a peep
Was I better for it?
Introspection only deeper?
Or is this the beginning of a downfall
One destined for a true bottom of the self
Only time will tell as I make my bed
The sun has not even set
Yet my eyes are tired of being open

Not Myself

I don't feel like myself

I am not myself

I am a prison looking backwards

With the future locked off

I want to run away

But feel bound tighter than ever

I can't keep doing this

Home

It was never home
It was never a place you felt solace
It shouldn't have mattered
But somehow it did
Home
A reflection of the person you love
No mere manifestation is needed
No physical attributes given
Only a feeling, a sensation
One which never came for you
Looking back, it could have been any place
Any place for me as I was holding your hand
But not for you
There was only one
Only one spot you wanted me in
Free to wipe clean off a dirty slate
One tarnished by where we were
You saw the torment it could cause
Simply within my soul

Technologically Shamed

It's like a reverse progression

A perverse justification

A remorseful relocation

From a snapshot of ill-advised intent

Walking forward 10 steps

Backwards 11

Damn technology

Keeping this close

Even though they are easily so far

No more photos please

No more posts on the subject

Delete delete delete delete delete delete

In Between the ground and the sky

I once had this dream of finding something of substance

I became too floaty for those on the ground

Too grounded for those in the sky

It was a strange place

Where not many occupied

Searching for days turned to weeks, months, and years

There is no you to finish this story

But the story is not over yet

Made to be blind

I was angry
Angrier than I have been in a long time
The dejection was just too much
I lost my cool
Punched the fridge
My hand felt broken but I knew it wasn't
Grabbed my bike
Sped off like I had something to prove
I was angry
Angrier than I have been in a long time
But at least I felt something

Trash Day

Your discarded filth

Fills my lungs with rancorous feelings of sensational sublime smells

I can't stand to look at the gorgeous items you've ruined

Destined for a fill of land poisoned for all time

What would the buzzards think of your actions?

Their gizzards wiped of any kind of decency

All because you couldn't finish your plate

Plastic is the enemy of progression

Brightest Bush

Your bright green tendrils greeted me with life

For over 20 years I watched you grow

Thanks for providing a base during games of tag

Some shade in the summer

Even floral sweetness for the bees

A home for the birds

I'm sorry it had to end for you today

I wish I could have given you longer life

It's selfish that I cut you up

But I hope you forgive me

I will forever be glad for the times we shared

Rest easy old friend

Sleep Well

I can't shut my eyes

But I don't want to see

Your visage is broken beauty

It hurts my soul to stare

I've done my best to match the way your ghost floats in my mind

It's not very kind

The way you keep me up at night

Just repaying all those past indiscretions

Part 2:

Work
or an incompletion of progress

Weddings

Weddings…
God damnit I hate them
What a complete waste of resources
Save your money
Buy a house
Give yourself a good start to life

Starting life together with a loan from one day of bliss
The rest just stress
How ridiculous

And we do it to ourselves
Mr. Brightside

Look at you fools
Rambling on to *Mr. Brightside*

Drunken messes
Huddled together

Truly disgusting
And I am forced to sit here and film this like I give a shit

Who is more pathetic?

The genuine losers basking in their former glory
Or the man wallowing in his misery writing poetry at a crowded dance hall

This Week

This week was shit
Filled idle time with stupid tasks

Waiting for the day to end
Watching each minute turn

And then a week from now it will be busy as hell
No time to think
Or take a break

This lifestyle is shit
I can't wait for it to be gone
In the Car

The car turns off
But not ready to go inside

Could just sit in here all night
The seat is comfy

Could just recline it back
Go to sleep for the night

Listen to music
Relax

But knowing that there is a door to go through
One with responsibility and challenges

Seems like a hurdle so hard to climb
Grab the keys

Time to go

At A Wedding

I've wanted to tell you for a million minutes
That you aren't for me
But I am a coward

Blame Blink 182
For romanticizing finding the girl at a rock show
The person who isn't real

But that is ideal
The chase
Not the destination

I love being on the hunt
As much as I may say I want to settle down
It is all lies

Please never believe me
No matter what
Never think it is what I want

That is night time me talking
In the morning I won't care
In the morning I will want you to go

That is just who I am
And maybe if you make it a second morning
Or a third

At some point you will just want to go
And you will hate me
Forever

Someone else I made memories with
That I can't speak to
My heart just can't deal with that again

And I don't wanna break yours

Vacation

I'm a vacation not a destination
Just because I sound nice

Doesn't mean you can stay here
Or hang out as long as you want

It just won't work out
Sorry to disappoint

Maybe the way I lure you in isn't fair
The lies I craft

Making myself sound like the perfect person
Only because you told me the thing you wanted

It is easy once you draw the person out for me
Then I can just become that

You chose to come here
After a few trips

Doesn't it all start to fade away
Laws of diminishing returns

But then you can't see me anymore
And your heart breaks
But vacations aren't permanent
Remember what I said at the beginning of all this

Crying Outside of a Taco Bell

Why were you crying outside of Taco Bell?
Did you see my face?

Was it really worth all that pain?
Just to lie to those around you

Or would it have been easier to just be honest
And let that burden go

Now you are all alone
Hunched over yourself

Crying outside of a Taco Bell

And I am just some guy at a red light
Seeing your anguish
Writing a poem about it

Thank you

Lines

I don't wanna be here
I don't wanna be here

I just need to see them
I just need to be touched

Comfort me while I'm sleeping
Hold me in my daze

Whisper in my ear
The way I should live my life

Control my active movements
Convince me with a knife

How hard can it be?
To go on living free

How cold can it be?
When I'm swimming six feet deep

If only you knew the person
I could always be

I wish I could love you
But that is just a dream

Young Artists

As an artist you build these worlds and dreams up from the dust

And usually once you are done crafting

Building

Molding

They get crushed

But once in a while someone sees your potential

Someone sees your gift

To what capacity that carries you is down to chance

Or maybe some strange luck

The key is keep building

Stubbornly so

The naysayers will overwhelm you

The belief may die down inside

The dust from defeat

Can be built back up

You just have to push onward

Be strong, young artist

Be curious, young thinker

You can change the world

You can show the people

Despite all the defeat

Your day will come

Cycles

The first time you do something everyone loves it
So you feel good
The second time you do something everyone starts to judge
So you listen
The third time you do something everyone starts to ignore
So you start to question
The fourth time you do something almost no one cares
So you stop doing it
Then everyone asks you why
And you make up an excuse
The only difference in breaking this cycle is nominal success
Then people pay attention

Art

There is no value in this game
Fools carrying more fools
Pretending to have knowledge
Self-appointed compatriots lying through their teeth
I hate your seething commentary
I hate your vicious smiles

It is one thing to study your discipline
Another thing to have a lack thereof
If I could turn my back on all of you I would
I am just fighting through the loneliness

Once I have my bearings straight
The compass set
I will be gone
Gone to create

Then you will absorb me with open arms

Part 3:

Sex
or some kind of release

Girls

I love every girl that doesn't give a shit
Mainly because I know they will be hard to get
They will see past my little mind games
And I love that

I want them to sit on my face
I want them to tell me I am not good enough
I want them to not cum one bit

But god damnit they are so hard to get

Bliss

I felt the most euphoria
Getting high and eating you out for hours
Your pussy was always so smooth and delicious

You sucked me off just right
And then we would pass out together
In bliss

When I awoke you were gone
And God was that perfect

Late Night Caller

Late night knocks at my door
Do nothing but feed my ego

When you lie down on the floor
What am I supposed to do?

I am just a compass
Without any sense of direction

Leading you into the woods
After you get your satisfaction

Maybe the wolves will get you
Or maybe you can ward them away

I hear taking your clothes off is a distraction
That's something in the dark you can do so well

Sheets

Girl why do you give up sex to get him under your sheets

Your nightmares will subside with time

That need to be held will fade with time

But you are better than anything he could ever give you

Love yourself first

How Many Times

How many times must you see me before you can let me go

She whispered

How many times?

How many times must you touch yourself thinking of me?

She whispered

How many times?

How many times must you tell other girls that you love the music I introduced you to

She whispered

How many times?

How many times must you drunkenly message me with no response before you take the hint

She whispered

How many times?

How many times will you waste your breath saying my name

She whispered

How many times?

Dance with Me

We are victims of circumstance
Loving the motions

Feeling the emotions
Feeling the debauchery

Come grind on me
Feel the love

I wanna fuck you
Will you suck me off?

Who cares
Enjoy the jams

When is tomorrow
So far

So, let's get it
Tonight and now
Friday Night Massage

Men like me get massages on a Friday night
When we need companionship and have none

Men like me pay $200 for a happy ending
When we think no one else wants us

Men like me touch a girl who has been touched a thousand times
by a thousand other men
All of whom paid to be jerked off

Men like me come back home living with our poor decisions
And stare at our bank accounts the next day

We think of all the other ways we could have spent that money
But on a Friday night we paid to be touched

We paid to be loved
We paid to just cum

All so we could escape that crushing feeling
That no one else wants us

And that no one else ever will want us
For at least a long while

Middle-Aged Woman

Middle-aged woman on the dancefloor
Dance away your pain

Tonight, you go home alone
Too drunk to feel the sadness

But tomorrow you wake up alone
The come down being harsh

Tears on your cheeks
I hope the high was worth it

Naked on the Beach

Time to feel better
Laying down in sand

Letting the sun drench my naked body
I feel so at peace

Those people all around me
Might as well not exist

This is just my time
My time to burn away

I want to turn to sand
And return to the Earth

Find peace in all that I took
Find solace in this small sacrifice

I use so many things
So many people

Do I deserve anything nice?
Will anyone read these lines

My naked body now clothed
How can I continue on?

IDK

I am only heartbroken by those that deny me
I know somewhere they could have been the one

Even though it is obvious they're not

I wish I could give that same time
To those who truly love me

But instead I push them aside

The last girl who really loved me
I couldn't even fuck

That's for no other reason than it was too easy

I want to blame my ex
But she is long gone

It is on me I know this

But I really can't change who I am
Deep down inside

Maybe I will fall for the right girl

Or maybe it will just be years of casual sex followed by pining over people who don't matter

Ghost Ship

Easy target
Snuck into your parents' house
Watching Ghost Ship
We made out
The other girls giggled
I was absorbed into you
Not sure what was fat and what was a breast
I had felt your warm embrace
You tasted nice
It was cold
Fun night
We all walked around
Made out some more
Then I got picked up
You texted me
I never responded
Not sure where you are now

Seek Me Out

Swallowed too many tadpoles to breathe
Swimming in my stomach tell them to leave

Grab my cock tell me to perceive
All the pretty punches you will weave

I will gladly accept the torture
It makes me smile

And laugh uncontrollably
And laugh uncontrollably

I am a sick freak on the same plane as you
Just find me three rows back

And life will never be the same
Hate and love you

Beautiful mess
Baby blessed
Hands outstretched
Shove your whole being on my face

Cramp my style
Mold me so well
I want it
No more thoughts

It is great
Living in naivety
Not Sure

Where does it come from?
My mind wanders away and I just spill

It's a habit of moving my mouth
Except I am silent

Am I clever enough for you?
Having no more things to say

I thought if I stopped having casual sex
It would give me less to write about

But here we are
Ranting on a page

This is going nowhere
Goodbye

Horror

Girls filled with horror
Love my frail body
Because it is close to death
A walking skeleton of life
I give them my essence
And they leave me more brittle

I am simply in hibernation
Concealing what is left
Pouring this tired body
Into all the art I can
I will die behind the camera

It will be magnificent
You will remember

Sugar Rush

I see you there
Flopping and flailing all over
I laugh and stare
You amaze me in the worst ways

I wanna take advantage of your daze
And bring you home
But I won't
Because I know it would be wrong

Belly full of sugar
My eyes widen at the rush
And it feels so good
I just want this

I want it without the consequences
Preservatives flood my veins
And I crash crash
Cut my tongue out so I can't taste

Let the sugar die
Let it slip away
Someone else suffer from it
I don't want it

And you know what
I don't want you either
Go home you drunk skunk
Seduce me another time

I'm leaving

Avert

Avert your eyes, love
So, you can hide from the true feelings
The fact that
I could save you from your husband
And take away the pain

Curiously connect with my neck
Because you want to give it all the attention
Only to escape from fate
Falling into my world

Meet me in the stall
I Felt Nothing

I felt nothing
A genuine emptiness
It was supposed to be different
Your kisses were like any others
Sure I had a physical response
My erection was constant
But nothing else came
Am I broken?
Am I dead?

I'm not sure what to say
Not sure what to do
It was just hollow
Bullets with no gunpowder
And then you left

Frustration

I was hard

I was hard for a while

Anticipating your arrival

It was known

It was known leading up to everything

Sex was what this was about

So frustrated from a day of missed opportunity and squandered time

I should have been in Ocean City

But that might have been a waste of time too

Who knows?

You are here now and we are making out

I thought you might smell so I say let's shower

I make up some reasoning like I've had a long day

I'm still hard

Showering together

It feels nice

Finally laying in my bed

Was hoping to 69

But you are too big

I touch you to see if you are at least smooth

But no the hair is there

So it isn't going to happen

Guess we can just fuck

You mention condoms only
I oblige but know the moment is lost
I try anyway but I get soft as quick as I was hard
Then we talk…
Well I talk and ramble to scare away the awkward silences
It's been a while, I say I'm tired
You say you want to fuck again
It isn't going to happen
The smell despite the shower was too nasty
Your larger exterior just not my type
I couldn't keep going with you
You leave with neither of us being satisfied
All because of I

Touching Needs

Sometimes I need to be touched
Not by you but another
It hurts me to feel this way
Sadly though it's true
I fight these cravings
Especially at night
They will overtake me though
They always do
I will run away
Have my cake
Eat it too
Come back to you
Are you aware
Of what I do?
I'm not sure
I'm just broken
Deserving no part in your play
Forgive my weak body
Forgive my weak mind

Sex and Love

I don't want to have sex
I want to fall in love
But my main motivation is sex
Once it's complete I want to be alone
I push you away
And you fall in love with someone else
Is anything love, then?
One moment you could say you feel for me
But when I don't fulfill your needs
You move away
Was I supposed to live?
My true self wanted you gone in that moment
Was it as simple as pretending?
Are we that desperate to commit?
I guess I am
All I'm doing is looking for simple pleasure
Once it's gone and filled I want to be along again
Alone and away from you

Part 4:

Death
and all the consequences as a result

Heroes

All my heroes are dead

Well the ones that made a difference anyway

Because they aren't heroes until they die

That's when I need them the most

Maybe it is just guilt

Because I didn't give them enough of my time when they were here

Or tell them how much they mattered

If they are just energy now returned to the Earth, will they ever know?

What if the last thought before they died was, I wish you spent more time with me

Then my hero saw me as nothing more than disappointment

Toenail

My toenail was trimmed down too short
And it started to bleed
I kept digging down further
And it continued to bleed
I took it down to the root
Now my toenail is completely gone
I like this oozing red toenail better

Consume

Each generation has a mouthpiece
A slow leader that emerges

Drowning the minds of those who follow
Leading into a pool of thoughts

Thoughts to buy and consume
It is the same thing

The formulas
The algorithms

They change
They alter

But there is one
For each subset of people

The outcasts, the preps, the jocks, drug addicts
You aren't safe
You can't escape

We are all victims
We are all in it together

Why

We were all just kids
Watching shows that got in our brain

So now we dress like the people we worshipped
We became those figures on the screen

Were those who created doing it for passion
Or was it just to turn the economy

Now we are so disillusioned
Lost in a sea of stuff

Buy another box
Spend your money

Become this thing you are not

Anxiety

You smoke for anxiety
Anxiety because you smoke

The world is full of hardships
And this is how you cope

Just push a little harder
Maybe you will see

An end to the struggles
A fading of anxiety

Grow

Why don't you grow?
Not enough water? Too much?

Is the soil poor?
Do you have enough sunlight?

I wanted you to be so much more
But you just aren't

Maybe some fertilizer
Nothing?

I don't know what to do

You are changing into the same thing
The same thing as those around you

A little extra color doesn't change it
The frame is the same

I wanted you to be so much more
And you just aren't

Float On

Float on
Ghost boy
Float on

Do you
And float on

No one will know where you are
Go through the wall

Maybe a ghost girl will show up
Are ghosts even real?

How many ghosts will there be?

Anyway, float on ghost boy
Float on

Sparrow

Dead sparrow on the pavement
I want to find you a home to rest

But don't want anyone to judge me
For lifting your spirit up

To your final home
To rest

Why did you die
What happened

How can I help
It doesn't matter
Melancholy Moments

I don't want you around
In these melancholy moments

I don't need your voice
In these melancholy moments

You won't like what you see
In these melancholy moments

You will fall out of love with me
In these melancholy moments

We shouldn't see each other
In these melancholy moments

We should just part ways
In these melancholy moments

I can't see your face
In these melancholy moments

I just need to be erased
In these melancholy moments

Stray Bullet

The taste of blood
The iron taste of blood

Surrounded her mouth
As the bullet went right through her face

It was a stray
A stray bullet from a nearby altercation

Out of all the angles
And all the positions

It could have taken
It found her face

Now I just looked down
At her mangled corpse

Blood eking out
Flowing all around her motionless body

I wanted to touch it
But I couldn't

I saw her eyes glint my way one last time
And it was beautiful
As if all her essence was leaving through those two eyes
The beam of light struck me deeper than anything I have ever seen

Then she was gone
It was surreal

Little Worm

Little worm on the pavement
Left stranded from the heavy rain
How can I help you?

I'm walking and it is really inconvenient
For me to stop and pick you up
Put you in the grass

I mean would you fix my tire
If I was stuck on the side of the road?
Probably not

I will do you this solid
But you owe me one
Don't stray too far

Emotional Misunderstanding

We have lost so much
So many emotions misunderstood

Simple acts of kindness gone
And it shocks us when we have something genuine

But we cling to it
What we feel is real

Even if it really isn't
We will trick ourselves

Then the damage just goes deeper
Our souls sucked dry

When will it change?
Or will it slowly get worse?

Festival Vibes

I'm in an oasis of bodies and blood
Hormones raging
Drugs taking hold

Smoked up even
It's harder than ever to feel how I felt
Many years ago

It is fun
But I am already good to move forward
Is it bad that my attention is more divided?

Not by any lack of trying
I just wanna listen to music on a personal level
By myself in a dark room at night

But with you, friends, I will dance
Playing pretend
For as long as I can

I Miss

I miss Lexi
I miss seeing her wagging tail
Her excitement when I woke up
Or walked through the door

I miss her barks
Her silly ways of running down steps
I miss her love

I miss my friends from high school
Late night drives
With the radio blasting

We knew all the new bands
And yelled out all the lyrics
Eating junk fast food

I miss being at my parents' house
Sleeping on the third floor
Seeing the view of the waterfront

I miss my ex
Despite all the drama
She was my first

I miss so much as the rain pelts my half-finished home
Melodrama aside, I wish something was here
To help me see past the pain
Of missing so many things

Lexi

There are so many things you are going to miss
This house being done
Meeting the person who will be my wife
Possibly having kids
Watching me grow old

I wish you could see them with me
You were my buddy
Always by my side
I feel lost without you

Yeah you could be a pain
Yelling when I'd walk out the door
But that excitement when I came back
Nothing could replace that joy

I wasn't always the best to you
And for that I will forever be sorry
But I just need you to know how much I cared
Because I always did and always will

You kept me safe
You helped me conquer so many silly fears
With you I felt protected
Even when I didn't need it

All you ever asked for was affection
And treats
All you ever needed was me
I was your world

I hope your final moments were peaceful
I held you as close as I could
You know I will never forget you
And all the happy memories you gave me

Dance Around Little Girl

Let go little girl
Let them cover your eyes in diamonds
Flower petals made of gold

You are free now
But you own someone something sometime
Just remember when they cash out

Dance now
Dance high on whatever prescription pills they feed you
Seeing all the colors or lack thereof

I'm sorry you don't see the world as it should be
I'm sorry I can't save you from their grasp
It's just a matter of time

I know you will call out for me
And I won't be there
Because I saw you when you were dancing

I was the one that started pushing you down from your clouds
It was the snake that pulled you down the rest of the way
Maybe I just couldn't stand your happiness
Maybe it made me feel better when you were broken

But never forget it was me that shattered your soul

Demographics

Oh he acts so self-destructive
Jumping from extreme to the next
Little else he doesn't know

Just a puppet on a string still
He fits nicely in the gap
Between single and married

Just another demographic
For us to cater to
Let him be sad

Let him push people away
It's good business for us
Little does he know

What is he doing over there?
We don't really care
As long as he still spends and busy useless junk

Keep on supporting
Keep on dying
Keep on breathing

Until you can no more
Don't worry, we'll replace you
Remember you're not special

Dreams

I keep having dreams where I am dying
Who knows why?
It's kind of cool though I guess

Because I wake up still alive
And that is nice
I feel like I will die young

Before I reach my full potential
That terrifies me
Or just rotting away along

I won't know until I fall asleep though

Steal Me Away

Always so much time to rape my soul
Suck it all away
Make me smile through a screen
Pretend nothing is wrong

Gotta be PC
Through a PC
Lots of thoughts to run through
Process the bits

I want to climb out
The content speaking for itself
Maybe if I stuck it out
But I burn out

They want you to fade
Chasing a dragon
But never getting it
How does it feel
Must be nice

I just wanna go home
Really go home
From 15 years ago
Maybe more

It was simple
It was easy
I was a brat
It was blissful

Judgement Days

I see the things in you that you'd rather not hear
I see the spots in which you are going to age
I can tell the parts of you losing strength
I sit and judge your appearance
If we grew old together it would be the worst thing
There have been too many others I have seen shriveled up
It will happen to you
And I won't be able to love you anymore
I will grow discontented with you
And I will not be happy
I sit and judge your appearance
As if mine is not just fading too

Circle

I lost my tribe
The people around me

Now I skip
On stones

Trying not to drown in the water
Without looking down

But I am an island
Nowhere to turn to

Hoping maybe someone will save me
I'm trying not to pay for sex

I'm trying to avoid a massage
The temptation is hard

These are my drugs
The things to quit

What will make them go away
Will it ever stop

A cycle a circle
It's what I am caught in

It's been so many years
It hasn't stopped

Even if I wanted it too

Moon Sky

The sun is coming up
But the moon is still deep in the sky
The shades are singing purple
Asking me why

Are you breathing toxic air?
With a stench of death
Are things clean and pure?
Lilies growing everywhere

I don't know what to say
I don't know what to do

I wish I could draw
Maybe it would help me see you
Some version of perfection
Stuck on my side like glue

The moon is gone now
The sun burning bright
Another lovely day of heat
To warm my soul, preparing for the darkest of nights

Toy

Steps taken away from you
That divine distraction in the sky

What can I say
That hasn't been said?

Words are meaningless
In that tiny head of yours

Shaped my mind against the treasure trove you dug up
All glitter with no value

How can things ever go back
I'm a broken toy in a world of flesh

Just let me die
Just let me die
Just let me die
And never cry

See You

Come to my arms
Sit down on my lap
Breathe in my shoulder
Take your nap

The pain is gone
The waves are calm
Daddy's gonna relax you
With your last song

I hope you find peace
Wherever you go
Hope you find love
In a final show

This is for your own good
The sickness is spreading
Without daddy's kiss
So many things you'd be dreading

Goodbye for now
But not forever
You're quiet now
I think I'm clever

Die

I'm gonna die one day
And that's ok
Tell my mom and dad
I lived like it was yesterday

All the green fields are grey
All the toadstools have faded away
Soon my eyes shut wide
Soon my heart stops racing

Repeat

I smell lavender
I see darkness
Nowhere to really go from here
Thank you thank you thank you
Tombstone

My tombstone marked a major blow
It was a last call to arms
I heard the whispers of the horses
In a long-forgotten twilight

Marry me in front of him
May the kisses be so sweet
As if it was him you truly had
Because of circumstance

I go into the windy night
I go into the dirt

Time Stamps

I could just not be here
Tomorrow

I could just not be sitting here
Tomorrow

When all the pain melts away
Today

When all the thoughts enter my brain
Today

Your lack of talking hurts my soul
Now

Nothing having words to speak out loud
Now

Might make me go away
Forever

Might make you cry always
Forever

Self Death

I used to watch Dexter's Lab

And now I am spending nights

Scoring hand jobs at Asian massage parlors

It is the death of the self

I can't even finish

Another 100 dollars wasted

I come home

To an empty space

All alone

Convinced this is Hell

Sure of it

Just keep moving forward

Even if the soul is dead

Lay down

Fall asleep

Maybe it will be different tomorrow

God

God is dead
He died creating man
Putting his all into us
And we swallowed him whole
Leaving nothing behind
Now we have to be better

School children with no teacher

250 Dollars

I could pay a girl 250 dollars to act like my girlfriend
250 dollars
To act like my girlfriend
I could slit my wrists for zero dollars
Well actually a few bucks if I need to buy a knife
But I have one in the kitchen
Funny how that works
Hard to stay in
Easy to go out

Iron

Ulcers fill the voids where your kisses used to be
Gums recede and show the whites of my teeth
I can taste the iron
Green mouthwash turns brown from the mixing of the blood
The pain isn't stopping
I can taste the iron

Days with Lauren

Days with Lauren

Were long

Early starts to make her coffee

Long nights trying to stay up

She ran me ragged

My energy level could not keep up

My sex drive nowhere close to hers

I was tired

I was stressed

She wanted to be a business partner

But was lost in how to help

The constant need to venture out

The mood swings galore

Days with Lauren

Were long

And I really do not miss them

Change (Or Lack Thereof)

People don't change kid
I'm here to tell you upfront
That girl you fancy down the way
The way she is today is surely here to stay
It won't get better
Might get worse
Things may happen
Life is an unpredictable farce
But one constant I know
Is that these people around you
Will never be any different than how they are right now

Thinking Back

It has all lead up to here
This very instant
Where I am writing to you
Reflecting on every life choice
Watching you live out yours
Do I have regrets?
Of course
Will you have them too?
For sure
Can I be there smiling with you?
What would that mean if I was?
Like I said here we are
Living out these strange choices
Forced to be separated
Forced to be alone

Acid Stain

Your skin covered my mind
Until I manifested into the nightmare of your soul
I was an acid stain
On the sheets of you and me
Collect me in the bucket of time
Rusted and affixed on your mantle
I will be no mortal's prodigal sun
As you abandon your bed post
Leaving me to rot
Proving the point to the masses
It was all just wasted energy
Looming deep in the madness of the written word

Growth

It grows to touch a night sky
Longing not to die
Only small bits of oxygen
Make it feel so high
It continues fading upwards
Longing not to die
Helpless as it may be
Struggling to survive
Longing not to die

Part 5:

Love and the complicated balance of life

Facial Structure

It's the facial structure
It stays the same

I see the faces of those I went to school with in their sisters
Their brothers

I see it and it takes me back
I see it and I find it attractive

I was shy and fat in high school
No confidence

But when I see that face, I think maybe I could have them
Since I have confidence and I am in shape

This is my chance to be with that girl
But then I have to remind myself they are 18 or younger

Is it a sexual perversion?
Or some kind of twisted claim for nostalgia

Either way I should stop staring
I should stop creating fantasies
The light turns to green

Candle

Burning candle on a shelf
Think of me and yourself

Bought when we were still together
Feels like you will burn forever

You will fade with those memories
From a love made just temporary

Recycle the jar you were in
For another day to win

True Love

Let's never get married
Let's go to a mountain somewhere without telling anyone
Scream our love from the very top
That way the Earth knows and that's all that matters
I can make you a ring made of brush and bark
Carved by hand
And when it becomes brittle and breaks then we know
Know the time for us to depart
Connect with a new soul and experience it all again
That way we can both be truly free
Avoid the trap that they feed us
And before we both die; I will find you
To say I love
One last time
Before you close those beautiful blue eyes
Returning to the Earth, who knows that was our final goodbye

Tired

I want you to look bad with makeup on
Bags under those tired eyes

At least it's real
At least it's pure

Who keeps you up at night?
Is it your demons?

Or the things they put in your head?

Cheat on me again
Tell me I'm not good enough when we fuck

At least I know it's real

So Close

You came from a place where everything was broken
I came from a place where I watched the broken come alive

You wanted perfection in everything
I wanted to see all the jagged edges

We could have met somewhere in the middle

This I see so clearly now

Why was it so hard to solve the puzzle?

The answers were right there for us

I could have fixed all the broken pieces
And you could have enjoyed the semi perfection I created

Hypnotic Call

We used to talk for hours
But I never saw your face

You wanted me to hypnotize you
So I played my part

Everytime I mentioned seeing you
There was an excuse

I did research and found out who you were
You were an overweight wannabe pastry chef

After I confronted you that was it

Years went by and you made the cake for a friend's wedding

Not knowing who I was you came to me
Asking why I was filming

Very rude but you didn't know me
I still wanted to get your attention

So then I tagged you on Instagram
Blocked

Never talked again
Now as I write this
I will probably look you up once more

Responsibility

Sleeping girl
Stay that way forever

I can get so much more done
Feel all that freedom

Make myself perfect
Act out my routine

Start the day slow
Productive
At my own pace

Then you wake up
Time to take care
Goodbye peace
Maybe more time tomorrow

Take

I give you my heart
Because I know you won't take it

I tell you I love you
Because you don't say it back

Play hard to get
Because it turns me on

Take all I have
Because I know you will enjoy it

Text Me

Text me all night
I won't respond but I want to hear from you

Send me a novel
Of your life's story

You know you want to
Then I can use it later

As ammunition to get under your skin
So, when it comes time to hurt

I can pierce through your heart
And leave yours right back in the little pieces I found

True Dreams

Dream on pretty girl
Dream of me

Collect all the good memories
Filter out the bad ones

Maybe when you wake you can forgive me
And we can talk like before

That would be nice
But if that happened it would be my dream

Party Girl

I put my hands around your trembling body at the party
You are high and having a bad trip

I kiss you gently on the forehead
Tasting the salt off your cold sweat

It will be ok I tell you
You stare back at me like no one has ever stared before

How do you know you say
I don't reply

But either way I am here for you now

Hands at Night

Hold your hand up high
Near your window

Maybe if I look closely, I can hold it
And make you happy

Just for one night
Is that all you need?

Or did you want more?
Because it's not **ever** a guarantee

Last Night

I wish I could give you last night
The lights the sounds

I wish I could have looked in your eyes
Screaming lyrics along with you

Could have gone hours with you
There by my side

So drunk almost falling over
But having the time of our lives

I wish I could give you my mind
And what I see when I see you

But you were so far away
And now it is morning

I stumble up
I can't find your number

Would I call anyway if I had it?

Woman with a Ring

I convinced a married woman to fall in love with me
She wants to leave her husband

I fucked a married woman for four hours straight
She told me it was the best sex she ever had

I now have to tell that married woman I cannot stay
After I made her think she could live with me

After I told her I could see myself watching her kids
And having a wedding with her

I am the devil or something beyond wicked
I just lure playthings in and have one magical night with them

I guess that is better than a life without that one magical time
It all degrades from there anyways

Pink Haired Girl in Walmart

Pink haired girl in Walmart
Your makeup was perfect

Your body immaculate
The baby on your arm just a mild distraction

From all the love you obviously had to give
Who pulled your life down?

And made you this way
I wish I could rescue you

And give you all you deserve
But what do you deserve?

I may love you for a moment
But I have to remember

You are just that pink haired girl in Walmart

Fingertips

I've always wanted to love you
Reaching out fingertips to your heart

I tiptoe on the surface
But brave no further

Love is a word
I use it too much

How can you believe me?
When it's so obvious it's a lie

It's been a year now
And I'm already tired of your face

I habituate too quickly
And this is just further evidence

The fact that you stay so loyal
Is nothing short of a miracle

I might be gone tomorrow
Or maybe some dumb thing will keep us together

Letters You Wrote

I just cannot have a single thing from you
Reading a single word, you wrote takes me back

And just wants me to think
That it could all work again

As if time apart fixes it all
I don't know why it would

I need a pink
On my brain

To snap me back in place
And help the realization

I need that right now
Or maybe if I text you it will bring us back

Forever

Hello Dolly

I went to every performance of *Hello Dolly*
Watched you in awe at every second

What a pure love we had
It was unconditional in every way

And then it started to get complicated
We began to fight

Over what I don't remember
I wish I could take it all back

I tried hard to love you
And you did for me

It wasn't meant to be
But what if it was

I guess I wouldn't have grown
But just fallen into you

And I wouldn't be here now
Dreaming of those days long passed

In A Target

To the girl
In the black dress
At Target

You were perfect
My true soulmate
I just know

I had so many chances
To say you were gorgeous
But I could not muster the strength

I regret not saying
All the things
I wanted to say

We passed by
So many times
And it was fate

I should have said it
I should have said it
I should have said it

If you read this
Know you're perfect
In every way

I wish you could be mine
I wish you could be mine
I wish you could be mine

Damn
I met my soulmate today
In a Target

Years Ago

Everyone I met
About two years ago

Is either married or having kids
Here I am with neither

Still playing on the same dating apps
Talking to the same kinds of girls

Filling their heads full of lies
And making myself sound cooler than I am

Somehow, I forget those women
And then I remember them again

When I find their profile
There they are with a new man

Not too long after I left
And it seems to be their one

Will I always be a stepping stone
Will I always just be their last heartbreak

Where does this all leave me
Where do I go from here?

Predictions

I will be 35
A professor
When I fall in love with one of my students

She will be 20 or 21
Love older men
And will think I am so great

It will actually work out
And our love will be secret
Until she graduates

That spark lasting
Keeping our attention
But life will hit

I won't see that glimmer of youth anymore
And I will get bored
There might be a kid

Now 42 seeing a girl half my age
We will fall in love
And I will leave the first one

That pattern will go as long as life will let me
And that will be as close as I get
To some sort of true love

The Movies

Remember going to the movies dude
It was sacred to us
Special

Every trip was an adventure
All this hype in our minds
Spending the day talking about it

It was always a great time
And one I will never forget
Because it was time with you

Dream State

Last night I was in your room
More like an apartment

It was filled with things on shelves
Things that were symbolic of you and I

They were filled with dust
The place was a mess

It was filled with people partying
Mainly girls

All of whom I wanted nothing to do with
They were instantly judging me

I had to pee
But the toilet was broken

I used it anyway
And then I left

Not before the girls said things about me
Under their breath

I went back outside
The streets were wet and it was raining
The last thing I remember
Was thinking of how the time we spent was fun
But it was never meant to last forever

Then I woke up

Inspire

Expression is love

Express yourselves

But do it uniquely

Sit for hours

Thinking of how to be different

Let the content flow

But do it creatively

We are all capable of so much power

So much raw energy

Don't get distracted

Don't get distracted

Don't get distorted

That is the key

Prove me right every day

Make something great

Make it today

Generations

We are no different

From those who came before

The styles may change

The words may differ

But we are the same

It is no surprise that change won't come

The rebels are disposed of quicker

We may think we are more connected

But the disparity is true

Somehow though we remain

Voices need to be heard

But the screams are just louder

Making our work ever more tedious

Making life that much more difficult

How can things be changed

My thoughts may never reach you

The person I'm destined to meet

I will never see you

In this swamp of self-defeat

But continue on forward

Please

Break these chains

Leech

Tip toe while sleepwalking over my dreams
Your rosy red cheeks make mine turn blue
My brain cannot function
My eyes roll back
Sleep is where I find a reprieve
But you find me again
Making me sweat
Until exhaustion sets in
Then how can I replenish my body
You truly suck life out of me
But I love it
I need your rows of teeth sucking it all out
Like an engorged leech over my eyes
Let go when you are full

Mountain of Doubt

Maybe I loved you because we never met
Or simply because you rejected me
Now I see you as a challenge
Wanting to prove to you love exists
I could take you to dinner
Buy you flowers
Climb that mountain of doubt you cast over me

Then when it is all over
And you finally accept me into your life
I will slowly back off
You will be baffled
It won't make much sense
But I will disappear

And it will break your heart
I will be another reason
For you to never trust again

I'm sorry

Text Poetry

A dream of a long distant night filled her mind
Although she tried to clear the fog it was no use
There was no excuse for the lack of verbal
Execution on his part she finally had enough and
Asked him politely to leave only to dream that
Same dream for the rest of eternity

Text Poem 2

Every line written
The beauty undone by man.
Every machine created
Made by his hand
Recycled words cannot compare
To the originality expressed in you just sitting there

Companionship

Is a fear of loneliness
A motivation for love
That's really it
Just hoping to have a person
To pass the time with
A selfish want
But a timeless need
An only desire
A fleeting feeling
Why are you here?
Then please come around
Not for too long
Only when I make a sound

Go Away

What I can't have
What I want
What is too far
What I want

Only space is good for me
Only distance means the love
Longing makes the heart pound
It is an easy barrier

If you were around
Everyday
You would not be missed
You would not be longed for

Easily dismissed
And forever
Would not be cared for
Go away

Make my mind race
Go away

Make the time break
Go away

My Time

I have these dreams of seeing your face
And I have these nightmares of being with you
Peaceful times reading you books
Stressful times of fighting
You are a love
Also a liability
Making things beautiful
Times of a messy house
Giving me purpose
Sucking away my soul
A million other things to do with my time
Are you even worth it?

At the Movies

One seat away in the theater

Said you were uncomfortable

Sat in the chair next to me

Watching anime like I was 16 again

I saw our legs crossed the same way

We chuckled at the same moments in the movie

It was cute

Started to think maybe it was a build up

To something more

Made me yearn for a companion

But then you and your friend left early

It was ok

But maybe if we had talked

You looked too young

You, her, she, it, me, my, love

I could scream a thousand whispers of hate at your face
Spew out ten million legs to wrap up your body
Cut your face to an unrecognizable mass
But it wouldn't change anything
It wouldn't bring back a past
A past filled with silly faces
Late night embraces
Loving moments
Holding hands
Thinking this was it
We had it all
A kiss to seal
Hearts to steal
You moved on
I'm still trying to
That's the simplest way I can say it

Blood Rush

Words could not describe the range of things I feel
Blood rushes through, making my veins congeal

Your presence makes me blush
Body makes me weep

The soul won't conceal
What the heart cannot keep

You Were A Doll

You were a doll
Made up from scrapped wood and metal shavings
Splintered from the pieces that made you whole

You were a doll
Devoid of diminishing thoughts
That made you weep precious tears

You were a doll
With a face that could never see things close
Only distant objects floating by

You were a doll
Wanting nothing more than just to die
But life was flowing endlessly through your veins

Ruse

It was there from the distant haze
The face struck me so fruitfully
I wanted to ask you all your thoughts
Knowing what makes you happy

Those features so unique
That beauty truly one of a kind
I'm not sure if I will ever hold it
But having this time with it

Might be all that is ever needed

My words are now translucent
Caught under prying eyes
See right through this ruse
As a smile graces each part of your lips

Swear

A malicious beauty
Comes from the solar flare
The one you swore was harmless
Brings death to us all

The tides may rise
The winds will howl
It will be ok
It is most foul

Your recycled soul
Takes place in two fields at once
Rising through wilting sunflower petals
In a landscape more brown than green

They could not see what I did
As the bushes broke back down
Only rain soaked tears were shed
Oh to see that simple frown

Family

We start a family

To escape the sadness of losing our own

Missing the home cooked dinners

Ones spent with our parents

We look back and weep

For a while just the company of friends

Is enough to tide us through

But soon the need for substance

Pulls harder than anything else

So we settle down have a child maybe more

All to recreate the nights we once shared

Staving off the reflections of the past

To prove a brighter future

Let it be known

Let it be known

That she was too preoccupied with the contents of her left breast pocket

To be aware of the jester in her court of lies

Let it be known

The rules were stricken down on this day

The same as the living of the peasant kings ruling over their kingdom of mud

Let it be known

That your ears deceive you reading words ringing in your mind

If only such a slate could be wiped clean

Maybe then the queen would retain the ownership she once had

Skateboard Girl

Skateboard girl push on
Let the folly of youth
Carry your spirit far
This may be a peak of innocence
Beware the traps
Beware the tricks
That straight tracks have twists
Turns
The unexpected
I know you will be ok though
As your long legs drift further away
Turning into a distant mirage
What is your name?

30 Years

I triumphed

I failed

I made it

On the cusp of 30 years

Surviving longer than my mind could ever process

It is the slowest flash of life

The quickest clock to reach one second

Things have just begun

While so many chapters have closed

A tear has been shed for lost youth

But a smile emerges for the timeless wisdom

I thank the ghosts

I thank those still standing

You've made me who I am today

For better or worse

I could never say a moment was wasted because each piece makes the whole

Stories cliché and unique

Bittersweet Berries

Bittersweet berries burst on your tongue
Hot air fills up your lungs

Cold perspiration consumes your flesh
While laughter sits here until your death

Repeated Listening

May you be healthy and happy all your days
God damn the times could be good right?
All those mornings in the sun
I loved every second of the happiness
Diluted down to its essence
It was all so great
Someday I'll be with you plays on repeat
My mind is so free
Dreaming of you tonight
Dreaming of all the what ifs
All the things that could have been

Pain Love Pain

All of it hurts

Even as I type my thumbs bleed

My brain cracks

It's the worst

And yet I enjoy it

That great rush

Of constant struggle

Happy sad happy sad

Take me down and lock me away

Because nothing is better than this

Crash Lips

It was like thunder on our lips
The way you showed your skin
Help me to fit in
It was a gift
Forever fleeting for the wind
You bled late into the night
While I hoped it would clot
You died
I did not even know your name
It would never be the same

Go get fucked up

I remember watching you get fucked up

I always enjoyed it

Seeing you slowly succumb to your demons

Making out in the corner of the room

Living in the filth

It was amazing

Take me there again

Let me be that voyeur

That beautiful soul burning slowly

What a rush

Waves

Somber waves carry me to separate shores tonight
Just a preteen boy preaching thoughts that never change
I'm a conundrum and you're a cliché
Together we balance each other out

Longing for Motion

A want to be colored in
A need to be fulfilled
Time turns on and desires falter
It was the clock that was wrong
You never aged a day
Looking on, I wasted away
Motion seemed too painful
Subsistence ran deep
Thinning bones with brittle skin
A voice without a room
A home without a place
Your light burned away my eyes

Yellow Dye

How could you notice the yellow dye?
It was glued to the tips of your nails
Dipped in a liquid
A liquid composed of chemicals
How is it different from the water?
Pouring out from the sink
The color is more appealing than that boring clear drink
Yellow invades your eyes now
It seems to be your favorite
If only I drank the polish
Maybe I could be your favorite too

Part 6:

This is it,
the closing part

An Ending

It's always trouble ending things
Never knowing the right outro
Perhaps it's easier to end things so

www.ingramcontent.com/pod-product-compliance
Lightning Source LLC
Chambersburg PA
CBHW021949290426
44108CB00012B/1003